MY LIFE AS AN EDUCATOR

What My Teacher Education Program DIDN'T Teach Me

CANDOUS S. BROWN

DEDICATION

This is for Grandma. Because, in her opinion, I was so smart and neat with everything I did. Because all I had to do was be "more better" and I would be successful. Because she was the first person that was willing to be my student. Because I will forever miss her and appreciate the sacrifices. Because the sacrifices she made shaped me into the woman I am today.

**I love you forever G.
Georgia R. Hall**

**1949-2016
I will forever give you Roses.**

TABLE OF **CONTENTS**

DEDICATION   II

REFLECTIONS   1

APRIL 14, 2015   3

THE BEGINNING   7

YEAR 1 - I HAVE NO IDEA WHAT I'M DOING   9
    The Things I Learned – Year 1 - All you must do is lose your mind one good time. 18

YEAR 2 – ANOTHER ONE BITES THE DUST   20
    The Things I Learned - Year 2 - You must establish a routine.........25

YEAR 3 – WHAT WAS I THINKING? 28
    Things I Learned – Year 3 - It's ok to start over..........................31

TRIAL AND ERROR   33

YEAR 4 – And then there were the girls   35
    The Things I Learned – Year 4 - It's ok to talk about yourself.........41

YEAR 5 – ALMOST REUNITED   42
    The Things I Learned – Year 5 - You don't have to like them to teach them. 46

GROWING PAINS   48

YEAR 6 – IT'S TIME TO SPREAD YOUR WINGS   50
    The Things I Learned – Year 6 - Your colleagues aren't always meant to become your friends. 56

YEAR 7 – THIS AIN'T FOR ME   59
    The Things I Learned – Year 7- Every grade level is NOT for you. ..64

YEAR 8 – Losses and Gains   67
    The Things I Learned – Year 8 – Sometimes the memories are all you have just to help get you through the day........................72

COUNT IT ALL JOY!   **75**

YEAR 9 – You Have to Lose to Win 79
    Things I Learned – Year 9- Not everyone is going to root for you. Some people want to see you fail. 87

MATURATION   **90**

YEAR 10 – It Really Was an Accident 93
    The Things I Learned – Year 10- Never forget that the students are ultimately in control of the learning environment..................101

THE PRODIGAL STUDENT   **103**

Blessings on Blessings 107

TESTIMONY   **110**

Scriptures and Quotes   113
    Luke 16:15...............................114
    Luke 15:7 119

Proverbs 9:6 122

Proverbs 12:1 124

Deuteronomy 8:3 128

Psalms 27:4 131

Philippians 4:6-7 133

Numbers 6:24-26 135

Genesis 1:1-3 139

2 Thessalonians 3:10 140

Joyce Meyer 141

Deuteronomy 31:6 145

James 1:2-3 149

2 Corinthians 5:7 153

Galatians 6:9 154

1 Peter 5:6 157

CLOSING REMARKS   **161**

ABOUT THE AUTHOR   **169**

REFLECTIONS

February 13, 2019

As I sit and contemplate my next steps, I can't help but remember the things I actually did learn while taking my educational courses. I learned to plan lessons so that I could present information to the students in a way that is coherent and orderly. I learned to meet the students where they are so that I could then challenge them to go further than they ever anticipated they could. Most of all, I learned to be present because any situation can become a teachable moment.

The things I hold dear from my time in Christian Brothers University's education program are that I must be a(n)

1. *Servant Leader- In order to effectively reach my students, I have to own and appreciate the fact that I am providing to them a service. I must be to them what I would be to my own child if I were to teach him.*
2. *Effective and Reflective Practitioner- In order to effectively provide services to my students, I*

must not be afraid to reflect upon my practices and ask myself what did or did not work. I must be willing to change and adjust my methods to meet the needs of my students.
3. *Champion of Individual Learner Potential- Speaking of students' needs, I have to know and understand that individual students learn and process information in different ways. I must reach them where they are with materials and exemplars they understand before I can challenge them to go beyond their current state.*
4. *Builder of Vibrant Learning communities- To reach my students, I must maintain an environment that encourages students to first come to class! Once I get them into the room, I must engage them in ways that are meaningful so that they will want to learn and understand the materials I am presenting.*

All of this I learned while at CBU. I will forever appreciate my educational experience at that institution because I was encouraged to look at students holistically and not just as a data point.

This is why I do things the way I do.

APRIL 14, 2015

I woke up with a lot on my mind.

I've gone through so much over the last several years. Most of the stress I've endured comes from my career. I've shed so many tears. I've conquered fears. I've been lied to and lied on. I've suffered such heartache and felt tremendous pain. And it hasn't even been a decade. I truly think all of this took place in the first six months of my career!

But as I approach the close of my seventh term in the classroom, I've had an epiphany. Through everything I keep coming back. People always ask me why. When I vent, I seem to have such horrible stories. Of course, people ask why I come back! The answer, though, is that I truly love it! Not only do I love my career, but I also feel that this is my calling. I feel like I was chosen and appointed to this important position. Over the years, God has equipped me and strengthened me so that I can continue to do His work. With that being said, I don't preach to the kids as I teach them their lessons. But

I do try to instill in them some life lessons. And over the years, the same kids I've fussed and yelled at have come back to me expressing their gratitude. They may not remember the lesson on comma usage; they may not recall the time I attempted teaching sentence diagrams (HOR-RI-BLE). But they do remember the times I pulled them aside and had heart to heart talks with them and gave them hugs and told them my door would always be open for them should they ever need to come in. Some of them still use that "door" to this day.

So with that being said, it was put on my heart to write a book. Something practical and honest that would display what I've learned over the course of my years in the classroom.

In its pages I will reveal how I survived (yes, SURVIVED) the academic school year. So, without further ado, I will reveal my secret...

The Word of God. Daily I have read the Bible and certain scriptures and verses have touched my heart and given me peace. I have taken this peace with me into the classroom daily. Although I vent my frustrations, it is truly the God within me that has helped me to endure.

The book will be divided into seven sections:

1. In the Beginning
2. Trial and Error
3. Growing Pains
4. Count It ALL Joy!
5. Maturation
6. The Prodigal Student
7. TESTimony

Section seven will have scriptures that I believe have helped me during the most tumultuous time of my life—BECOMING and BEING an EDUCATOR! I truly believe that everything I have gone through up to this point has been shaping me and preparing me to do this.

God's hand is ALL OVER THIS ENDEAVOR!

I hope you enjoy reading it as much as I have enjoyed writing it!

THE BEGINNING

The beginning of the school year is always so exciting. As a teacher, you're coming up with all these different lessons to engage the students and get to know them. You're deciding how to decorate your classroom, how to arrange the desks. Should the students sit in groups or rows? Where is the classroom library going to go? What is a cool way to display quality student work?

In the beginning you come up with the best strategies. You are idealistic and want to try all kinds of new things. In the beginning, you see the blank slate. You see the potential. You are truly aware of what you are doing, and it is all done with a purpose. The best thing about the beginning of the school year is that you are rested enough to think of all these great and wonderful things to try and implement.

The beginning of any endeavor can bring about so many emotions. My first days of the school year are always filled with a bit of anxiety and fear. I'm afraid I won't teach the kids enough information; afraid I won't be able to relate to them. I'm afraid I won't have enough time to help them grow. I'm afraid I'll lose my temper. I'm full of fear that I just won't be good enough.

The thing you must remember about the beginning of the school year is that fear and anxiety are natural. It signifies that you truly care and are conscious of the ways in which things could possibly turn out. You have a bit of forethought and you are playing out scenarios in your head. This is all good.

YEAR 1 - I HAVE NO IDEA WHAT I'M DOING

I never wanted to be a teacher. From as far back as I can remember, I wanted to be a doctor. More specifically, I wanted to be a Trauma Physician in the ER at a major hospital in my city- Memphis, Tennessee. I was obsessed with biology and anatomy. I would watch The Discovery Channel and The Learning Channel religiously. My mind was a sponge ready and willing to absorb anything that pertained to science, nature, and life. There was a reality television show that would air when I was a kid called *Trauma: Life in the ER*. I was in elementary and middle school watching these heroic doctors and nurses using their knowledge of the human body and medicine to save lives. I wanted to be one of those heroes.

The summer before I started my freshman year of high school, I participated in a program at University of Tennessee Medical School in Memphis, Tennessee. There we performed science projects, such as animal dissection, and learned medical terminology. We were given stethoscopes, white lab coats that had the school logo, name tags, book bags that contained medical literature, and so much more. That experience solidified it. I knew my future and my path- I was going to be a doctor.

In high school, I took courses such as Honors Biology, Honors Chemistry, and Anatomy and Physiology. I never made less than a B in those courses. I struggled in Math, however, and could often be found in after school tutoring before heading to cheer practice. Although I had some difficulties, my passion never waned.

I graduated with honors from Millington Central High School in May of 2003. The following August, I enrolled to be a freshman at Christian Brothers University. I must confess, CBU was number two on my list of colleges to attend, but I don't regret attending that institution. It truly provided me with an education that ensured that I would be successful in any walk of life.

My freshman year was rocky. I hated many of the courses I was taking. I struggled in my beloved Biology and Chemistry courses, and sadly, by the end of my first semester, I was placed on academic probation. What an unfortunate start to what should have been one of the most carefree times of my life!

By the time the second semester of my freshman year began, I had dropped Biology as my major and boldly stated that I was Undecided in what my future endeavors would hold. Let me tell you, that decision was by far one of the most liberating I had ever made up to that point in my life. It allowed me the opportunity to explore different types of classes and truly discover what I really loved. One thing that was a constant in my life was a love for reading and writing. I began taking multiple English and Literature courses along with multiple Psychology and Sociology courses. Finally, I began to thrive.

I loved my English and Literature courses so much that I eventually declared English as my major. In May of 2007, I graduated with a Bachelor of Arts in English. But I had to ask myself, "What was I going to do with an English degree?" This was the million-dollar question that was posed to me at least a dozen times, but the truth of the matter was I didn't know what I was going to do.

People said I should apply to law school or get a corporate job. But the fact of the matter was I didn't want to do either of those. Law school would be entirely too stressful. And honestly, I had no intention of arguing for a living. Anyone who knows me knows I'm a crybaby. I would get in front of a judge and jury and make a complete fool of myself. As for Corporate America... NEVER! Business suits and a restrictive cubicle with no windows was not for me. I don't like "boxes" so that was a no go.

Not only did I not know what I was going to do with my degree, but I had also become pregnant my senior year of college. I now had the added task of trying to find answers to two important questions-

What was I going to do with a degree I never intended on getting, and how would that degree allow me to raise and provide for my son?

So, there I was, five months pregnant, a new college graduate, and unemployed. I had some serious decisions to make and only a few short months in which to make them. But after months of deliberation, coaxing, and prayer, I finally choose my path. I decided to go into education. This decision was not something that I came upon on a whim.

There were so many tears shed because I KNEW that I NEVER wanted a teacher's life. First, I'm not a morning person and I never have been, so that 6 to 6:30 a.m. work arrival time automatically made being a teacher the absolute LAST profession that I EVER wanted to be in. Not only that, I remember how some of my classmates behaved in class… the immaturity, the noise, and the smells. How could I possibly consider having a teacher's life?

In the summer of 2008, I applied to be an educator with Memphis City Schools. I was scared. I was nervous. I was confused. I was about to be exactly what I never wanted to be- a teacher. The fates had dealt, what I initially thought to be, a cruel hand. But I successfully made it through the interview process, and in the fall of 2008, I began my first year as a teacher.

I had no idea of what to expect. At the time, a stipulation of being hired was that I must immediately enroll in a Teacher Education Program. Not wanting to ruin an opportunity, I began the process of acquiring my teaching licensure. However, the fact that I had majored in English made me highly qualified to teach the subject within the district. It was for this reason I was hired. I began teaching in my own classroom before I'd had any formal instruction in educational theory and methodology. To say that I was ill-prepared in many regards is an understatement. I didn't know the prescribed curriculum; furthermore, I had no idea where to find it. It wasn't until my second year that I discovered the curriculum map for the courses I would be teaching. The courses I would be teaching were English II Honors, English II Standard, Etymology, and African-American Literature- keep in mind this is all during my first year.

    The fact of the matter was I was overwhelmed. I had taken Honors English II in high school, so I basically taught things that my own English teacher taught me. There were limited resources for African-American Literature. Luckily, I still had the text from my own college level course. From that college level text, I chose works and created a custom book for the class. As for Etymology- I had NEVER EVEN HEARD OF THE TERM LET ALONE THE SUBJECT! So, I was studying those materials and creating lessons as I went. What I learned on the fly, I would teach to my students. The classes I taught were at maximum capacity, and the students were beyond unruly. To top it off, I was young and small. If it weren't for my attire, I could have easily been mistaken for a student- a blessing and a curse that added to the learning experience.

    My first year in the classroom was beyond difficult. I was sick a lot; I was stressed; I lost weight; my hair fell out; and I wanted to quit. At one point, I would have. If it had it not been for a student stopping me, I would have quit right there in the middle of the day. I had made up my mind that I was going to leave and never come back.

One particular day, I'd finally had enough of the disrespect. I'd been cursed out by more than one student. Due to my stature, a couple students had even walked up on me to try to intimidate me. I decided I was done. After dealing with this for months with no real assistance, I grabbed my purse, my phone, and my keys and I walked out. I had no intention of returning. They could keep everything I brought into the room: the posters, flower arrangements I'd made, the books I'd created. All of that could stay, because I was done. I was in my car with the key in the ignition about to put it in reverse, when there was a beating at my window.

A teary-eyed girl stood there looking at me with pleading eyes. To this day I have never forgotten her. She said to me, "Please don't go. We won't have anyone else." That was the first time I realized that all it takes is one student to sway your heart. I went back into the building and found a note on my desk from another young girl. To this day, I still have that note. I have continued to read it over the years. In the letter, she encouraged me to be strong and not let the actions of a few students stop me from educating the ones who really wanted to learn. It was at that moment that I realized I was not going to impact every life in my classroom. Realizing that truth, I put it together in one simple thought- if I impacted at least one child, then I could impact the world.

The next day I went in with a new attitude and a new resolve. Due to the actions of one brave student, I was changed forever. Thanks to her, I still hold on to the same resolve and attitude today. To be a teacher I don't need to impact all my students. That is a dream of all teachers, but I must be realistic about the world in which I teach. All I need to do is impact one student and my job will be worth it.

The Things I Learned – Year 1 - All you must do is lose your mind one good time.

The school in which I taught during my first year was not for the faint of heart. There were more than enough fights. Students tried to fight me. Students got in my face and cussed me out. I was so stressed out that my hair fell out. I had to cut it to even it out. Not only that, I miscarried a pregnancy. I was sick a lot. It was a rather miserable experience. Things got so bad once that I literally picked up a desk and threw it across the classroom.

Now, I don't recommend allowing yourself to go through the stresses that I went through. I also don't recommend throwing desks. I do recommend that you set expectations early, so that you don't become fed up and have to result to drastic measures like I did. If you don't want students on the floor unless they have express permission, say that and have an appropriate consequence for the breaking of that rule. If you don't want them yelling out answers, establish that. If you want them to have certain things for your class, express that. Not only do you say it, follow through with the consequences of not following those rules. Be fair, firm, and consistent. Students will respect that, and you won't have to lose your mind like I did.

YEAR 2 – ANOTHER ONE BITES THE DUST

I was "surplused" from the first school in which I taught. Basically, what that meant for me was that I was too inexperienced. It is a way to fire teachers without firing teachers. You are put on a waiting list for other principals to possibly choose you as a teacher for their schools. I was fine with that because I had no intention of returning to my previous school anyway. Teaching in my first school was enough to make me reconsider teaching altogether.

The summer following my first year was long and stressful. Because I was surplused, I had to find another teaching assignment. By July, I still had no prospects for a school. Without any teaching hopes, I was considering my options. While in college, I worked at Walmart and Sam's Club, so I considered reapplying and attempting to obtain a managerial position. It wasn't my best plan, but it was a plan nonetheless.

The very day on which I was going to go apply at Walmart, was the day I got the call from the board of education. A person from human resources stated that she had found me a school placement for the upcoming academic year. The call came on a Friday. I met the principal of the school on Saturday. I decorated my classroom Sunday. I reported to work on Monday. It was a quick turnaround, but I was thankful to have a job. I honestly didn't want to go back to Walmart or Sam's. In my eyes, any new teaching assignment was a welcomed task.

The only problem was I had no idea what to expect. I was going to be in a different school in a different part of the city. Not only that, I would also be teaching two new subjects- 11th grade English and 12th grade English. I'd have to learn as I go.

To add to the confusion of a new school and new area of town, I would also be driving from a new address. During my first year in the classroom, I lived with my parents. However, sadly, a few months into the new school year we had a quarrel that changed everything. And because of that, I packed up to live with my grandparents temporarily. To this day, I don't believe they know how much it meant to me for them to open their home to my son and me. Were it not for them, I would have never gotten my masters or my teaching license.

At any rate, that was not the only stressor I faced that year. My infant son was now a chunky toddler who was approaching his "Terrible Twos", and I was taking a full-time course load in my master's program to get my teaching license. It was shaping up to be a rough year, and that's an understatement.

The mentor I was assigned really wasn't of much help either. She only wanted me to watch and imitate the things that she did which was not my style. The principal and many staff members were under the impression that I didn't want to be there. But none of them really asked me about myself or what I had going on outside of work that made things difficult for me.

A typical day went as follows:

- *Up by 5a to shower, dress, and eat breakfast*
- *On the road no later than 6:15a because it was roughly a 45-minute drive from my grandparents' house to the school in which I worked*
- *From 7:15a until 2:30p I'd be on campus teaching. If we had meetings, I'd leave campus no later than 3:45p*
- *Monday through Thursday from 5:45p until roughly 9:45p I'd be in class. So, I'd leave work, grab food, and head to my college campus (they didn't offer online courses back then). More often than not, I'd study or take a nap in my car until it was time for class to start as it was too far of a drive to go home and then make it back to class on time.*
- *I'd make it home by roughly 10:45p and prepare to start all over again the next day.*

When would I have a personal life? When would I spend time with my family? My friends? I was miserably exhausted. I remember one particular night where we were taking a break during the class and I fell asleep- in class. That was unheard of. My favorite professor at the time was so worried about me that he called to make sure I made it home safely. So, you see, it wasn't that I didn't want to be at the school to which I was assigned. I had quite literally taken on more than I could muster.

And not one time did anyone at the school ask what was going on with me in my personal life that made me seem so distant and withdrawn. We are encouraged to make a family like atmosphere in the classroom for our students so that they can thrive, but shouldn't the same be done for the teachers so that they can thrive as well? Even without the professional support I needed, I always knew my purpose.

I rarely smiled at work until possibly the second semester of the school year. By then, my classes had subsided and I was a bit more rested.

But I knew that after it was revealed to me that it seemed that I didn't want to be there, that I wouldn't be asked to return- no matter how good of a job I did.

Truthfully though, I wasn't a good fit at that school. I didn't participate in anything. I was unable to attend activities due to my class schedule. And overall, I needed to be with my son more. To top it off, I just never really felt comfortable there. Once again, I was surplused and found myself looking for a new teaching assignment. I just couldn't catch a break.

The Things I Learned - Year 2 - You must establish a routine.

Students thrive on consistency and routine. If you want them to come into your classroom immediately and begin the warm-up, practice that. If you want your papers to be passed to the front of the room and then to the right so the student on the end can place the work in the appropriate file folder,

PRACTICE THAT. The students won't know what you want them to do unless you say it, show it, and practice it. This is how you build classroom routines and procedures. If you want students to have certain jobs or tasks, say it, show it, and allow them to practice it. If these things are done at the beginning of the year, it will be easy to maintain. If you introduce these things while the students are new to you, they become the expectation.

As I previously stated, many people at that second school assumed I didn't want to be there because I was not very active. However, what they didn't know were the things I was going through outside of the work place. You must find and keep a support system. Even if that system is outside of your "prescribed" support.

My mentor only wanted me to do things her way. On another hand, the Reading 180 teacher was more approachable and understanding. She and I built a bond and when I had questions or wanted to vent or needed help with my homework, she was a willing hand and a listening ear.

Administrators may not know you personally, so they may assign you a mentor based on seniority. This is not always beneficial. If this happens, don't be afraid to step up and ask someone for help but only if you are comfortable with that person. Don't get angry about the mismatch. Teaching is a practice, not a science.

YEAR 3 – WHAT WAS I THINKING?

Being surplused from yet another school gave me some clarity. I was neither upset nor discouraged this time around. I learned that every school isn't for me and I am not for every school. So, I set out to determine what I wanted in a school home. Conversely, I set out to determine what I could offer my new school home.

I was young and ambitious. I was also a very willing learner. I had already taught three grade levels and two elective courses. Going into my third year as an educator, I thought myself to be a bit of a commodity. But I also knew that I had so much more to learn.

In June 2010, as part of my search for a new school home, I attended a job fair at the board of education. I didn't know what to expect or what schools would be present. I just went and hoped for the best. Actually, I prayed with all my heart. I asked The Creator to send me somewhere that I would be needed. Somewhere that I could grow and help others grow. I asked to be guided to a place that would allow me to be impactful.

I walked into the auditorium ready to accept what I'd asked for. I looked professional in my pant suit, carrying a folder that contained my resume and cover letter. As I looked around and tried to steel my nerves, I heard a familiar voice say, "Hey, Candous! How do you feel about coming back to the Bay?" I turned and saw a familiar face. She had been the assistant principal at the school that had been my first teaching assignment. To say I was a bit shocked and on edge is not enough to convey the full breadth of my emotions. But something inside of me urged me to hear her out.

I went to the table where she was standing, and we exchanged cordialities. It was then that she let me know that she was no longer an assistant principal. She had been promoted to principal and was given her own school. This could be the opportunity I had prayed for. I made my decision that day. I would not wait. I would start my third year as an educator in my third school. I would fix up my third classroom, and I would attempt to make my third year the best one yet.

I was excited. I would be teaching 9th grade English with Etymology and Creative Writing as electives. I would get to teach The Odyssey, Romeo and Juliet, and Greek Mythology. I was in love with the curriculum- especially now that I knew what one was.

I was a part of a ready-made team. We were the Freshman Academy, and it was awesome. The support I received from my teammates that year would be unparalleled for several years to follow. We had a system that worked. We had speakers come in, took the kids on field trips, and incorporated tutoring into our daily schedules.

We were truly a family, and the students could feel our bond. I knew I had found my forever home at that school, and I was so thankful. I was so afraid to go back to the part of town in which I started teaching because of unpleasant memories of a particular place that I almost missed out on the opportunity of a lifetime.

All schools are different. All staffs are different. Even schools that are in close proximity to one another have completely different cultures and climates. Had I not taken the risk of going back to that area, I wouldn't have met the kids and people that have shaped my teaching style even to this day. Sometimes, you must go out on a limb and try new things so that you can find what is right for you.

Things I Learned – Year 3 - It's ok to start over.

There have been times in my class where the routines have not been mastered by the students and they behaved as though they did not know what was expected of them. It was at those times that I would tell the students to stop what they were doing, gather their materials, and exit the classroom into the hallway. Since they didn't know or understand their roles as students, we were going to start the class over and practice things until they got it right.

    This may not be for everybody because of the time it takes away from the lesson, but this is a valuable thing to do when necessary. First, it shows the students that you mean business and there are non-negotiables in your class. Second, it establishes control and order in your classroom. It's not that you are showing them that you are the boss, but you are showing and telling them what you expect of them. This is directly related to your classroom management. Don't get frustrated. Just start over and tell them why you did.

TRIAL AND ERROR

The beginning of each school term is a time to try something new. You incorporate new strategies. You learn new material over the break, so that you can teach an old lesson in a new way. Sometimes, you must revisit old lessons and review your notes. In this way, you can see what did or didn't work. This method allows you to "perfect" the lesson and increase the chances of student growth.

One must know and understand that there are going to be things that you try that won't work. To be honest, that's ok. It is all a part of the process. The first time I tried to incorporate Socratic Seminar in my Honors level classes was an EPIC FAIL! Nonetheless, I didn't give up. I tried the strategy again in class several times before the students seemed to get the hang of it. They all realized that Seminar was just a fancy way of saying we are going to have a class discussion. It's a matter of you trying until you get it right.

A teacher must be a reflective practitioner. Keep a journal of all the things you try to do in the classroom. You must keep a record of your lessons. Try to film some of them.

You have to see what it is you're doing. Not only this, but you also must be honest with yourself about what is or isn't working in your classroom. Don't be afraid to ask for help. Don't be afraid to try something again. Above all things, don't give up!

We all learn by trial and error. Teaching is no different. We have to learn what works for different types of students. We also must learn what works for us as educators. We can't be afraid to incorporate bits of ourselves into the classroom dynamic and atmosphere.

YEAR 4 – AND THEN THERE WERE THE GIRLS

On our quest to improve student engagement practices, my school administration decided to try a new strategy. It consisted of incorporating gender-based learning environments. My ninth graders left me to begin their sophomore year of English which would be taught in gender-based classrooms. One teacher would have all the girls. Another teacher would have all the boys. And this would only be done in the English class. Apparently, the students were so totally distracted by the opposite sex that they had to be separated to keep them focused. But that wouldn't affect me as I would still be teaching ninth grade English... or so I thought.

I found out about a week before the start of my fourth year that I was going to be looped with my students. What that meant was that I'd advance with them. Because I knew the students well, it would be easy for me to cater to their strengths, improve upon weaknesses, and build on what I'd started with them in their freshman year.

I wasn't excited. Granted, I loved those kids, but I wanted them gone! I enjoyed the ninth-grade literature, and I didn't want to have to develop all new plans for another grade level. I especially didn't want to teach a bunch of catty, chatty girls.

I did it anyway. Surprisingly, it was the most fulfilling year I'd ever had up to that point in my young career. The girls were fun, and they encouraged one another. They also kept each other in line. I didn't write one referral that year. They pushed me and asked questions. I pushed them and forced them to think. That was the year we read and acted out The Color Purple in class because they requested it. I earned their trust. They earned my respect.

In many regards, I never thought gender-based education would benefit the students. But there were so many things I was able to do with and say to them that I would not have otherwise been able with boys present in the class. We talked about life, boys, relationships, and safety. Many people would shy away from that. However, when they are confiding in me their personal issues, it then becomes my duty to protect them. Up to this point, the schools I had worked in had students who were transient, and many were in foster care. This made me want to protect them even more.

There was a young lady that I taught during that fourth year that was really having a rough time at home. She missed a lot of school, but I could never get a good contact on a parent to voice my concern. She was very outspoken, and everyone seemed to like her. There were a couple weeks when she was not in class. When she did return, I asked her to stay after class so that we could talk. I had to make sure she was ok.

In that conversation I found out that her mother's boyfriend had attempted to rape her. When she brought the matter to her mom, she was put out of the house. Other members of her family were either unable or unwilling to take her in, so she became a ward of the state. She was only in my class for roughly another week after that, and I never saw her again. Our students go through more than we can imagine.

Another young lady during that year was bullied by a staff member. She was in the process of allowing her hair to transition from a relaxed state back to its natural texture. As my students had witnessed my transition, I did the "big chop," I became her cheerleader.

However, when she came to me and stated that a male staff member told her that she was unattractive with her hair in its natural state I knew I had to do something. He told her that since she had an afro, no man would ever want her. I became LIVID! At that point, I was more than a cheerleader. I became her voice.

After that, I proudly wore my hair in an afro to show my support of her. Not only that, I confronted the staff member and told him if he so much as breathed her way he'd have to deal with me. These kids are at vulnerable points in their lives. The last thing they need is for someone to shoot down their confidence, especially when they are already lacking it. It becomes a teacher's duty to teach self-confidence.

On a high note, one of the best memories of that year was the research project. I asked the girls what they wanted to learn about. They proudly stated the history of the hair care industry, and I couldn't have been more ecstatic!

They worked so hard on those projects, PowerPoints, and presentations. It was also at that time that there was a young man that the other English teacher just couldn't get a hold of. So, without delay, he was placed in my class. The only boy with all these girls. They gave him the blues! Those girls showed him no mercy.

The lone male student came right in and got to work. He did his project on barber shops. I was so proud! When it was time for his presentation, he came in with a shirt and tie and after his presentation, the girls gave him a standing ovation. It was at that point that I realized that students were willing to work for me even if they did not work for others. I must take advantage of the respect they have for me and be careful so as not to abuse it.

Each of these young souls needed certain things, and I made sure I was able to provide it to them. It was this year that I learned that building bonds with students improves academic achievement. They won't learn from you if they don't like and respect you.

The Things I Learned – Year 4 - It's ok to talk about yourself.

Our students need to know that we are human. It's a great thing to intertwine the lesson of the day with a life lesson that you learned that pertained to that same topic. Of course, use discretion when including personal stories in your lessons. But I promise the students will appreciate it. Not only that, they will see how the skills pertain to real life. Now the curriculum becomes applicable.

During this school year, my girls learned the proper research skills while also learning about my journey and transition from relaxed, chemically treated hair to natural hair. I told them of my frustrations and the things I learned about product ingredients. Several of them have transitioned since this time. I am proud to say that the things I taught them may have directly contributed to that decision. Again, the curriculum becomes applicable. The skills they learned will be forever useful because of the one time I showed them how to use it in real life.

YEAR 5 – ALMOST REUNITED

Once again, I was looped with my students. With that, I followed them to their junior year. All of them. My classes were co-ed again and I was more than relieved. I didn't realize how much I missed the dynamic of having both male *and* female students in one room. It was definitely a breath of fresh air.

There was so much to cover that year. Students had to take the Discovery Assessment, the TCAP Writing Assessment, the ACT, as well as the End of Course Test. So much to do, so little time. I think the most memorable moments from year five come from the relationship I built with my co-teacher.

Our chemistry was undeniable. We fed off one another's energy and played up each other's strengths. Our teaching methods were unconventional, but they really worked. We split the week. Basically, what that meant for us was alternating teaching days. Two days a week she would teach grammar and writing. Two days a week I would teach literature. The remaining one day of the week would be spent in the lab working on keyboarding skills because for the first time, the writing assessment would be on computer.

We had to make sure the students were prepared. We made it work and the students respected us as equals. I do believe that not one referral was written that year. Year five felt like home. That was the year we became a family. And like many families, we endured major test that threatened to tear the family apart.

On her quest for the ever elusive "student growth data point," my principal brought in a new colleague to assist. Eleventh grade year, for students, is heavily tested and school scores are indicative of how well the juniors do on their exams. This new colleague was going to have a class of juniors to work with, mainly the "bubble students," to help bump them up. They extra help those students would receive could possibly help them meet proficiency standards on their exams.

Tensions ran high as students began receiving new schedules. They would be pulled from my class and placed with a new teacher. I wasn't happy about it and neither were they. Up to that point, I had been with most of the girls their entire high school careers. I had also been with most of the boys for half of their high school careers. So, it's safe to say that we were pained about the possibility of a separation.

The kids were frantic and distraught. I was angry because they were now MY kids. I felt like I had raised them and was unwilling to share them with anyone, especially a stranger. What could she possibly do for them that I wasn't already doing? It was a slap in the face. I'd been working my butt off with these kids only to have someone come in late in the game and take them from me and possibly take credit for what I'd taught them. I wasn't having it. And neither were they.

They gave the new teacher a run for her money. So much so that the new schedules were reneged, and the kids were able to come back home, so to speak. The catch, which is something to always expect, was that the new colleague would also become my "co-teacher."

It was awkward. I already had a co-teacher, and we had a system that worked. Now, we'd have to adapt and adjust to include a new person. We made it work for the rest of the year. The three of us formed a sort of bond- one that would be renewed several years later.

As an educator, you don't always realize the impact you have on your students. You don't realize how much you truly start to love and care for them, and they for you. Looking back on it, I was very possessive and overprotective of these kids because an "outsider" had come in. I didn't know whether or not she had their best interest at heart. I didn't know if she would care for them like I would, or if she would be willing to stay after school and work with them like I had done.

The last thing they need was someone pretending to be there for them. But we overcame it and our bond was made stronger for it. That was the year we found out how deep loyalties can truly lie. I will be forever in their debts for that.

The Things I Learned – Year 5 - You don't have to like them to teach them.

Let me tell you something, you are going to run across some students that irk your nerves. They are annoying on purpose. They are needy and do inappropriate things just to get under your skin. Some of them are going to push your buttons just because they WANT you to snap. Do NOT give them the satisfaction.

You must TEACH the kid- you don't have to LIKE the kid. But you also must be mature enough to not let that dislike cause you to treat the child any differently from the others. Think of it this way- you don't have to like your colleagues, but you do have to work with them. Do your job. Be the constant professional. Those are the students that are going to make you stronger in your career.

I say this because I know those students pushed the new teacher's buttons. I'm sure the pushing of those buttons is how the decision got changed and they remained in my care. I'm sure it was stated how horribly the children behaved and how the new teacher wouldn't dare teach them. So, the default became me, the teacher who initially had them on the roster.

Students should not know your personal qualms with them. That is utterly unprofessional. They should, however, know that you will champion their learning potential and that you are there to serve and meet their learning needs. That is the only thing that matters at the end of the day.

GROWING PAINS

There are going to be teaching assignments in which you feel that your growth is being stifled. People are going to tell you what to do, when to do it, and how to do it. Is that right? Of course not! As an educator, you should have the autonomy to do what you deem necessary for the growth of your students. But how can you do that when you feel that you are being micromanaged? When you are being told that your work isn't good enough? When the people in leadership positions aren't backing you up on the decisions you make for the students you know- the students with whom you spend the most time? When you are being told how to do your job? How can you grow?

Again, you must reflect on your own practices and encourage yourself. You won't always have a nurturing administrator. There will not always be someone there to pat you on the back. As a matter of fact, you will run across some people whose sole purpose in life is to test you to your limits and see that you fail. Don't you dare allow them to dictate your emotions! Don't you dare lower your standards because of someone else's insecurities. What the Devil meant for ill, God can and will turn around for your good. Keep praying. Keep fasting. Keep believing. Your faith will see you through any and every circumstance. Look to the hills.

YEAR 6 – IT'S TIME TO SPREAD YOUR WINGS

The beginning of my fourth year at my third school came with some challenges. My students, the babies that came to me as freshmen, were now seniors. This would be the first year that many of them would not have me as a teacher. It was so weird just seeing them in passing or only having them come to me for tutorials.

But there is always an upside to any seemingly bad situation. The upside to this was that I was asked to be a senior class sponsor. In this way I was able to stay connected with my kids and provide them with an amazing final year of high school! Even now as I sit back and reminisce on that year, I am brought to tears. I watched them grow up. How many people, aside from their parents, have the privilege of claiming that?

The most memorable times we had were the scavenger hunt, senior picnic, and prom. For the scavenger hunt, we took the students downtown to search for things that were characteristic and unique to the city of Memphis. The sponsors participated as well and we made it a competition. All day, downtown, running in and out of different places and taking pictures with random people in local businesses- it was so much fun! The kids were given prizes for the number of items found. They also were able to further bond with their classmates.

The senior picnic was a blast. The kids had no idea that their sponsors were plotting against them. We purchased and filled water balloons, and while they were eating or playing basketball or just lounging around talking and laughing with friends, we were planning to sneak up on them and attack! It was so fulfilling to see them running around and behaving like children. I honestly think we sponsors had a better time than the kids!

Prom was by far the most memorable thing from that year. In keeping with making this the best year ever for the kids, we allowed them to come up with the theme for the prom. After much consideration and a vote, the students decided on "Through the Looking Glass" as the theme. Of course, this did my heart good because I teach literature and Alice in Wonderland has always been a favorite. Due to logistics dealing with the future of the school, we would not purchase prom decorations- we would make them ourselves.

I can't tell you how many hours were spent after school in the basement and the art room making Papier Mache tea cups and saucers, cutting and coloring eyes and smiles for the Cheshire cat, and cutting and creating the deck of cards soldiers that protected the Queen of Hearts.

Their dedication to the theme was inspiring. So much so that other teachers volunteered their time as well. One of the coaches volunteered her time and money to build and decorate a "looking glass" that was used as a prop for prom photos.

Just thinking back on it, I have an overwhelming sense of pride about what we were able to accomplish. And the students were more than appreciative of our efforts to make their vision a reality. They had proven to themselves that anything is possible if they work diligently to achieve it.

Each of these things was made bittersweet by the news we received from the district. Sadly, the school was going to be fresh started and taken over by the ASD (Achievement School District). What was seen by the district as a way to help a struggling school was, in the opinion of others, a major door of hope closing. Instead of focusing on the needs of the community, a decision was made based on the data and scores of the students.

For many years, the school had failed to meet targeted proficiency rates in core subject areas. In my opinion, it was no fault of the students or teachers. The area in which these children are from has always been depicted as the lowest of the low. They didn't have access to resources that many other schools and students had. They were looked down on and shunned even by people who work(ed) within the district. By the time they got to high school, so many of them were already so far behind. The achievement gap had reared its ugly head and adversely affected these children.

My focus for them was and always has been growth. And they met and exceeded my expectations every year. But the state focuses on proficiency to determine whether or not a school should be on the "failing list." And as many of my students, and so many others within the building, were not meeting proficiency standards, the decision was made to shut the school down and reopen it under the ASD. The senior class of 2014 would be the last graduating class of the school as we knew it. We *had* to make it the best year yet.

The teachers would be given the opportunity to reapply for their positions. If hired, they would work for the new school and its new administrative team. Many teachers did reapply. I know I did. I recorded myself teaching lessons, submitted lesson plans and PowerPoints, went to interviews. It was stressful. On top of that, I was working with my two favorite colleagues to plan and execute activities for the seniors so that they could have a most memorable year.

I was offered a position. I could return in the fall as an English teacher in the newly renamed and rebranded school, but I turned it down. My kids, the ones I started with in my first year at that school, and theirs, were graduating. They would be leaving to start the next stages of their lives- and so would I.

I accepted a position as an eighth grade Language Arts teacher in what was considered a more upscale part of town. It wasn't that I didn't love the school or the area in which I had been teaching. It wasn't because I didn't love the kids- I didn't know then, but in the upcoming school year I would miss them so much that it hurt.

I left because I needed a change. I needed the opportunity to work in an area where no one knew me so that I could try new things. It is a blessing and a curse to stay in the same school for many years. On the one hand, you build a reputation and rapport with the students and families from that area. You earn respect as a professional in your field. But what people don't tell you is that there is some backlash. Students come to know your routines and ways. And when you attempt to try new strategies, you get a lot of push-back because people want to do the same old things. They aren't always willing to let you change. This was why I felt that I had to leave. I needed to grow. It was time for me to spread my wings and take a risk. But that was a decision I would soon grow to regret.

The Things I Learned – Year 6 - Your colleagues aren't always meant to become your friends.

Didn't your mother tell you that everyone isn't your friend? Apply that to the work place! No one should know what you are going through at home in your personal life. You never know who is gossiping about you. Keep your personal business personal.

Now, if you happen to run across a colleague that is genuine and becomes a friend, foster that relationship. You will need someone in the building to have your back. You will need a support system.

I'm not saying that you won't make friends at work. Some of the closest people to me are those with whom I work. What I am saying, however, is be aware of those with whom you share. Everyone isn't there for you. Everyone doesn't support you. Some people are looking for a reason to steal your joy and your shine. Don't allow a lapse in judgement to create a hostile work environment for yourself. Everyone isn't meant to be a friend.

Year six fully opened my eyes to the fact that everyone isn't there for you and everyone will not like you. The twelfth grade English teacher that year made it a point to let it be known to my students that she didn't like me. Not only that, because the students weren't keen on her, she wasn't chosen to be a sponsor which meant that all the things that I was doing with the graduating class, she was unable to fully participate in. Because of my status as a tenth and eleventh grade teacher, I would not have been on the committee if I had not been expressly asked for. Due to this, there was a lot of hostility and tension between us. So much so that on at least two occasions mediators had to be used. Now, I never tried to befriend this teacher, but I did at least attempt to be cordial. Sometimes, being cordial isn't an option either. Don't let that discourage you. Continue to do your job. The people who are meant for you will reveal themselves. They always do.

YEAR 7 – THIS AIN'T FOR ME

For the first time, I was leaving the high school life for middle school. I was going to be an eighth-grade language arts teacher at what seemed to be a very reputable school. I was excited to try something new. I knew I could be an asset. After teaching at every grade level in the secondary setting, I had no doubt that I would be able to adequately prepare those kids for high school. I was confident. I was self-assured. I was WRONG!

I was completely ill-prepared for the behavioral issues, the crying, the whining. These kids were babies. And most of them were spoiled babies to boot. I thought I would mold them into semi-mature, miniature versions of high school seniors because, technically, they were the seniors of their school. I have no idea what I was thinking.

I knew I was going to have to make some adjustments in my teaching style and delivery methods. I made my PowerPoints more colorful and kid friendly. I made my classroom colorful and cute. I bought cute chairs and a rug and made a sign naming my reading corner "Ms. Brown's Book Nook." I advertised a Book of the Month in my class newsletter and incorporated fun activities to complete after the readings. I was finally getting to be the teacher I wanted to be, or so I thought.

Every teacher on the eighth-grade team was either new to teaching or new to that building. This meant that we were all learning the administration, the culture of the building, and the students. Not only that, a neighboring middle school had been permanently shut down and now those students were coming to this new school with their own culture, climate, and issues. To state it clearly and unequivocally, I hated it.

The first week of school was such a shock to me. I've never had to walk to students to wherever they needed to go. I'd never felt so much like a babysitter in my career until I taught middle school. I knew on the sixth day of school that I would not be returning. I was not coming back to that building or to any grade that was not ninth grade or higher.

Nothing that I did was good enough for the principal of that school. The one compliment that I got was underhanded. You know, one of those compliments that starts off positively and ends negatively and makes you feel like crap afterwards? That was the highlight of my year. I was micromanaged, scored low, and all the time made to feel like crap. Not only that, after much turmoil within the eighth-grade team, the math teacher quit and was replaced by the previous year's eighth grade math teacher. I thought she was a very good teacher. She was very structured and stern.

Later, however, I learned how much of a bully she was to the kids and how manipulative she could be. She was throwing her teammates under the bus while making sure she looked like the only teacher on the team who was doing her job. Apparently, we didn't measure up to her standards. Not to mention she was very close to the principal and would report back things that were taking place- whether they were true or not.

Looking back on it, everything that took place that year seemed to be so that I could not get another job after leaving that school. The scores I received made it seem as though I came to work and did absolutely nothing. Nothing I did was right or academically sound enough for those students. That became a major contradiction when their state exam scores came back. According to the exam, an overwhelming majority grew in comparison to their previous year's scores. And that was all the validation I needed.

I left that school as a TEM (Teacher Effectiveness Measure) Level 1 teacher which is grounds for termination. I was, quite frankly, pissed off. I had never been scored lower than a TEM Level 3. I couldn't understand how nothing I brought to the table could be beneficial. I didn't get how the things I was doing were being deemed not only inadequate, but as being complete trash. I had to go.

Thankfully, and by complete happenstance, I ran into the principal of the school I was applying for and hoping to get a position. I literally begged him to look at my resume and my student scores. I urged him to see passed the TEM Level 1 score I was given because my student growth did not reflect that. I left him my contact information and asked him to reach out to me if he thought I was a good fit for the students at his school. I was more than sure that I would not be returning to that middle school in the fall.

Sure, enough I was contacted and invited to a job fair for an interview where I was offered a position as an eleventh grade ELA teacher. I had never been so relieved in my life. I was excited to leave the beast that is middle school and return to more familiar territory. The first day of school couldn't arrive quick enough!

The Things I Learned – Year 7- Every grade level is NOT for you.

Some people are great at the pre-K level. Others thrive at the elementary level. Still others find success at the middle or high school level. These preferences are based on personality, creativity, energy, and many other personal characteristics of the educator. Just because one person thrives there doesn't mean that you will. I taught at the middle school level for one year. NEVER. AGAIN. I knew on the sixth day of school that year that I would never again teach middle school. And that is perfectly fine.

Don't get discouraged thinking you are not in the career that you are supposed to be in. Try different grade levels and see what works for you. I thrive at the eleventh-grade level because of the fast pace and stress. Others can't handle it. You must find your niche and go for it. It just so happens that I've taught a different grade level every year that I've been in the classroom. I have that experience and I know what works for me and what doesn't. You must find that for yourself.

But while you're in whatever grade level you may be in, it pays to be organized and professional while you wait out the year until your next opportunity. My professionalism went to the extent of making copies of student work and filing it away-just in case. That "just in case" moment presented itself several times through the year while I was at the middle school level.

One student said that I gave her a zero because I didn't like her. In all honesty, I gave her a zero because she cheated on her work. I took a picture of her hand, where she had written the answers to a quiz, and put it in her file to show her parent. I also had a parent call the district board of education on me. The parent stated that I was deliberately failing her son even when he was turning in the work. In actuality, the handwriting on his assignments did not all match. Someone else was doing the work for him. Realize that at the end of the day, the parents will almost always take the side of their children. You must show proof of why you have done what you have done. Be organized. Be intentional. Be ready to defend yourself.

This "self-preservation" strategy was also very helpful when the eighth-grade chairwoman tried to make it seem like I wasn't teaching. I had proof of assignments and test scores. She would not be able to constantly say that I was giving students grades and not teaching.

Always and forever practice this one thing- CYA (cover your ass). No one will protect you like you. No one will advocate for you like you. Do what you need to ensure longevity in your career.

YEAR 8 – LOSSES AND GAINS

Back to life. Back to high school. Back to the familiar hustle and bustle of what I have grown to know and love about the educational system. I was finally back in my element.

New school, new year, new students. I couldn't have been happier. I was back to teaching eleventh grade ELA to kids who weren't still losing teeth or crying because they couldn't work their combination locks - yes that really happened. I was working in a building with many familiar faces. The principal had been my history teacher when I was a student; the assistant principal had been the track coach at the high school from which I graduated; one of the teachers in the self-contained classroom had been a classmate and childhood friend. It seemed that the planets had aligned, and I knew that it would be a great year.

However, sixth period would not let me be great. It's always sixth period. This class had some of the worst behavior issues I had seen in several years. They were loud, rude, disrespectful. You name the negative behavior, and I'm sure that class in some way, shape, or form exhibited it. To put it nicely, there were students in that class that were bent on making that class the absolute worst.

One class period, however, always gave me what I needed. They were funny, yet hardworking. They were chatty, but they stayed on task. In short, they made my work day worth it. There was one student in particular who made the class period worth teaching. The kids respected and looked up to her. She had such a sassy demeanor that we couldn't help but clash in the beginning. I guess we were just too much alike.

My first encounter with her was one that I will never forget. The students were taking ACT diagnostic assessments as junior year is the year for the ACT exam. I wanted to see where they were academically, so that I would know what to incorporate into my lessons to ensure growth. But for some reason, the students began talking during the test.

Everyone knows there is to be no talking during the real ACT and I wanted to mimic as close to a real test setting as I possibly could. After roughly 20 minutes of silent testing, the kids were ready to be done with the exam and they began talking. So, I said something to the effect of, "I need you all to be quiet. Even elementary kids know not to open their mouths during a test." The young lady who responded so sarcastically to me after that statement would go on to forever hold a place in my heart. She said to me, "Is that where you came from? An elementary school?" To which I responded, "No. I taught middle school last year." What she said to me afterwards, I will never forget. With a sassiness that I have never witnessed since- which included an eye roll, a slight tilt of the head, and a wicked smirk- she stated, "Well, maybe you should go back." I could only laugh and say, "I'll meet you there." I don't know what it was about her, but I knew she would end up being the one that worked the hardest.

The next day, the students were completing their final portions of the diagnostic. This same young lady came into the room, went directly to her seat, and began her task. During that time, she had some questions about the wording of a text. I think she believed that after the previous day's debacle that I would hold a grudge against her, which is why I believe she was surprised at my willingness to assist her with the task. From that day until the last time I saw her, we would have a bond that was unbreakable. I had gained her trust and respect.

Daily, before she would go to her vocational classes, she and a small group of her friends would come sit in my room to chat before catching the bus to attend their courses for the second half of the day. And that is exactly how it was the last time I saw her. February 11, 2016 is a day I will never forget. She and her group of friends came into my room to chat just as they did every day before heading to their vocational courses. We exchanged hugs and said our goodbyes and she said to me, "I'll see you Monday, Ms. Brown." That was a Friday.

The next day, Saturday, February 12, 2016, I was cleaning my classroom after dismissing students from my Saturday tutorial session. As I was cleaning, I found her binder. I remember putting it on the bookshelf near the door and saying to myself I would give it to her Monday. I thought it strange because she was one of those students who never forgets her belongings. But I shrugged off the feeling and put the binder away for safe keeping, knowing that I would give it to her the next time I saw her in class…

The following day, Sunday, February 13, 2016, I received the phone call that no teacher ever wants to get. My sweet girl had died. She had been killed in a car crash. I remember feeling sick and just sitting on the bathroom floor of my home screaming and crying. I couldn't understand it. I had just seen her. I had given her a hug. She had reminded me that her birthday was coming up and asked me what flavor cupcake I liked. I had found her binder under her desk and put it away so that I could give it back to her Monday.

Monday came. But painfully, she did not. I was fine until her class period came in the room. They were so eerily quiet. Her desk sat empty. All I could do was stare at it. No work was done that day.

For her birthday, I purchased cupcakes and balloons. I sat them on her desk and her class period had a party in honor of her memory. She would have turned 17 that day. It was another bittersweet moment that, unfortunately, many teachers will deal with in their careers.

The Things I Learned – Year 8 – Sometimes the memories are all you have just to help get you through the day.

As teachers, we never plan to go into the school year to be as close to the children as we sometimes eventually become. Yes, we hope to bond and show our passion- hoping that the kids we teach will, in turn, become passionate about the content. However, we never expect to build a relationship in which the kids begin to call you "best friend," "mom," "auntie," "big sis," or whatever term of endearment they bestow upon you. You never expect that sort of relationship, but you should never take it lightly. Building rapport with students is the one thing that will help you on your journey to becoming a great educator. You can know all the content in the world, but if the kids find you to be unapproachable or un-relatable, it's over. You may as well be trying to teach the wall to read and write.

The memories of the young lady we lost that year drove my students to be the best they could be because they knew that she would have wanted that. She stated it daily while she was alive. The memories of that young lady also pushed me to be a better educator.

I later found out that I was her favorite teacher because I was unafraid to be unconventional in the classroom. It is that memory that pushes me to continue to think outside of the box. I forever ask myself, "What could I do to make this more appealing to the students?" I also later learned that my lesson on Transcendentalism was her favorite. In that lesson I incorporated a song by India.Arie called "Video." After that lesson, her friends said that she would play the song on repeat.

It is not just the memories of us, the teachers, that remain with the students. We also hold memories of them so deep in our hearts that they become engraved in our souls. And sometimes, those are the only things that get us through the days in the classroom- because we know that one of them will hold dear what we are attempting to instill in them.

COUNT IT ALL JOY!

Being joyful during trying times is not always an easy feat to accomplish. This is the reason why we have so many people suffering from depression and anxiety in our society. These two emotions are also very prevalent among teachers and others who work in education. We take on the ills of society and try to change the world one classroom at a time- one student at a time. We take on responsibility for children that, in some instances, would otherwise not have anyone to turn to. It can be stressful and disheartening. We can become disenchanted and want to quit. But I am here to tell you that those trying times are here to make you stronger. You will become a better teacher, advisor, and mentor for it.

My favorite thing to do when I feel lost is listen to music, and I fell in love with the lyrics of a song that always reminds me that my trials will lead to triumphs. It is entitled "Count It All Joy". Credited to and performed by the Winans family, it has such a powerful vocal arrangement that one can't help but to allow the message to reverberate in his/her spirit. I always thought they were the Gospel version of the Jacksons, but I digress. I urge you to listen to the song and pay close attention to the lyrics.

This song has provided me with hope and motivation to persevere no matter what. To be joyful and give praise even in the midst of struggles. To smile and look to God even when the world is determined to defeat you. When the weight of life appears to be crushing your soul, you must remember that you are already on the winner's podium.

You have to really think about and meditate on the message that is presented in this song. We all go through trials and tribulations in our lives and in our careers, but those troubles don't last always. We must be thankful for the experiences that we are enduring as they will make us stronger and better. Not only will the experiences foster fortitude within us, but they prepare us for greater things in our lives. When things seem too hard to bear, you must know and understand that the Father will not put anything on you that He feels you cannot handle.

The enemy comes to steal, kill, and destroy. There are times in your life when you will feel that he has won. But know that through God Almighty you are and will always be VICTORIOUS! Praise God through your trials and tribulations just as you would praise Him through your victories and triumphs. Through Him you have the glory.

Cast your worries and your cares on Him. He is your counselor and friend. And once you lay those burdens down, trust in God and have faith that He will mend anything in your life that is broken. As I speak these words and minister to you, I also minister to myself because I am guilty of worrying about things that I know only my Father in Heaven can control.

Don't allow the negativity that can come with this job to burden you. You must look to the hills. Your help is not of this world. You can only do so much. The things that are not in your control, you need to hand over to God. He will give you the peace and understanding needed to endure your struggles. And once it's over, you will be stronger, more knowledgeable, and all around wiser for having gone through your storm.

YEAR 9 – YOU HAVE TO LOSE TO WIN

After the experiences I had in year eight, things could only get better. At least that's what I thought. In life, as we grow, we think we can handle the challenges that befall us. However, we forget that the challenges change us, for better or worse, by breaking our mold so that the new being that we are becoming is no longer trapped. Sometimes you just want things to be simple, but life is not simple.

The summer before my ninth year in the classroom, my grandmother was hospitalized due to complications with her diabetes. Eventually, because things were progressively getting worse, her leg had to be amputated. Daily, after my in-service trainings, I would go visit her as she recovered. Once she was deemed healthy and strong enough to do things on her own, she was moved to a rehabilitation center where she would learn to maneuver her new body. She was at her weakest and it pained me to see this woman who had always been so strong now seemingly so helpless.

All the while, I still had a job to do. I had to plan lessons, create PowerPoints, attend meetings, care for my son, perform domestic duties at home, and still find time to take care of myself. I was more stressed and worried than I cared to admit.

After several weeks, though, Grandma was discharged and able to go home. The family was so excited to have her back. But not even a week after her triumphant homecoming, she took a turn for the worse. I remember very distinctly the call I got that let me know she was being transported to the hospital. I was driving home from a student related radio interview. But I dropped everything to rush to the hospital to meet her there. Shortly after I arrived, my mother and grandfather walked in looking distraught. I knew from their faces that my grandmother would not be returning to us.

When the rest of the family arrived, we were taken back to a private room to receive word of her well-being. In hindsight, my sister and mother realized what was going on before the rest of us did. When the doctors came in and told us that she was not going to come home, it was as if time stood still. I don't remember breathing. I don't remember blinking. I just remember the air being sucked out of the room.

Everything seemed to be in slow motion. My sister fell to the floor screaming. My mother was trying to console her. I had to keep my wits about me. My mother lost her mom. My siblings and I lost our grandmother. My grandfather lost his wife. We all had a piece of our hearts ripped out of our bodies. If I can be honest, I've not felt whole since that day. It was August 16, 2016- a Sunday. Somehow, I went to work the next day.

The most consistent things in my life over the years have been my work, my son, and my grandmother. She would call daily at the same time to ask what I was doing. I would even put her on speaker phone, so the kids could say hello to her. She would ask what they were working on and tell them to be good and learn as much as they could. When the call didn't come, I was sick. But I would have been worse had I not gone to work. I just didn't want to dwell on the pain of losing my love.

I tried to maintain a sense of normalcy during the time that we were planning Grandma's funeral. I continued to teach. I continued to perform, but if I can be completely honest, I was broken. Life was so surreal.

I became depressed, and I tried my best to hide it. Unfortunately, it came out as anger. I was short-fused and unhappy. I cut myself off from those who were trying to be close to me. I just needed time to wrap my head around the fact that I would no longer see or hear from my grandmother. On top of that, my health began to decline because of the sadness.

As if dealing with the loss of my grandmother wasn't bad enough, I was now being targeted by the female administrator in the building. I felt like I could do nothing right in her eyes. It was as though she was trying to find anything to take to the principal so that he would either write me up or have me fired. She was constantly in and out of my classroom and was so rude to me. Not one time did she provide me with constructive criticism although she did one full-length observation and no less than four drop-ins.

I specifically recall an incident where she was reviewing my observation scores with me and she brought up my son saying that the students I teach deserve nothing but my best because they aren't fortunate enough to have the things that my son has. Little did she know that I was a single parent struggling to make ends meet. Little did she know that I was battling depression from losing my grandmother. She had no idea what I was going through and didn't care to ask.

Several months later, on my birthday, many of my colleagues wished me well and asked me how things had been going for me as they knew the relationship I had with my grandmother. They also knew how hard the day had been. When that same female administrator heard them speaking of my born day, she interjected herself into the conversation and asked how my day was. I really didn't want to respond to her because of how mean she had been. But I responded as cordially as I could. Just because she was rude to me didn't mean I had to be rude to her.

Apparently, she didn't like the response I gave because after it was given, she said, "Ok? It was just 'ok'? You were blessed to see another year and you have the nerve to say that your birthday was only 'ok'?" Of course, she couldn't have known what I was feeling as this was my first birthday without my beloved grandmother and I didn't care to let her know.

A few months later, I was injured and hospitalized. I let the principal know what happened and was assured that everything would be taken care of. But the next day, I was called by the financial secretary and told that I would be written up as a no-call no-show due to not putting in for a sub. I was in the hospital concerned about my health. The last thing I was worried about was what was taking place in my classroom when I couldn't even sit up or walk on my own.

I was sick of the negativity that was coming from her. I was tired of having to prove to her that I do my job. I was just over her antics. I finally went to the principal and made a complaint. I did not want her in my classroom again. I was not going to tolerate her bullying ways. After all I had done to get back to the high school level and work with a principal that I knew would support my methods, I was ready to leave.

I got my chance when it was announced that the school would be fresh started and made part of the Innovation Zone of schools within the district. I would be able to apply to other schools without penalty. Not only that, I could reapply to stay at my current school knowing that the female administrator would no longer be there.

The only downside to this change was that I would have to interview and prove that I was worthy of a job I already possessed. I didn't want to leave my kids and travel across the city to a new school because I worked so close to home. Not only that, I would have to uproot my son because I need for him to be near me as we are all each other has. But the process was taking too long. Positions weren't being filled. Teachers were leaving because the new principal had not yet been announced. It was making me physically sick with worry because of the uncertainty.

Even after the new principal had finally been announced, it was still another few weeks before decisions were made about positions. I couldn't wait for the new administration to determine whether or not I was a worthy candidate; I needed to secure a position quickly because I have a son to feed. So I accepted one at a middle school as an interventionist. At times, I regret not sticking to that decision.

Roughly a week after accepting the middle school interventionist position, I got a call from the new principal of what was supposed to be my former school asking me to not commit to the middle school because I was needed at the high school level. In all honesty, I didn't want to leave my kids. I had already stated I'd never teach at a middle school again, so maybe staying where I was wouldn't be so bad. At least this is what I hoped.

Things I Learned – Year 9- Not everyone is going to root for you. Some people want to see you fail.

In your career, you are going to run into people whose sole purpose, it seems, is to make your job hell. You can do one of two things: you can allow them to make YOU miserable, or you can continue to do your job to the best of your abilities and make THEM miserable.

I have never really been one to allow people to see me in a vulnerable state, and when my grandmother died, I took that mentality to a whole new level. It is that sense of pride over my emotional state that I believe made me a target for the female administrator in my building. It seemed that she took pride in kicking people when they were down. That is not behavior becoming of a leader. It's not behavior becoming of a decent person.

What I learned during this year is that you must have compassion for those around you because you never know the battles they are fighting. I had students who tragically lost friends in car accidents, to gun violence, and to suicide. As an educator, I can't reach them if they are in pain. I must first show them that I care about their emotional health before I can present information that I think is pertinent. When teachers tell kids that they aren't in the profession to be liked by them, they couldn't be more wrong. In fact, the more students like and respect you, the better they perform in your class. They have this inherent need to please the people they care most about.

We must foster that in such a way that eventually they want to please us as well as themselves. They have enough people in their lives telling them they will amount to nothing. We must prove to them that we care about and want what is best for them. We are champions of their learning potential and will do whatever it takes to positively foster their will and desire to learn.

MATURATION

Webster's Dictionary defines *maturation* as "the emergence of personal and behavioral characteristics through growth processes." Personal growth. When I was a child, I spoke and behaved as a child. As an adult, I have had to leave behind those childish ways.

I have run into many educators who have forgotten that just because we teach children it doesn't give us the right to behave as children. I teach high schoolers. I am no longer in high school. Now, that's not to say that you can't have fun with your kids, but you must establish boundaries and know when to have fun and when to get serious.

The things I've learned over the course of my years as an educator are to pick my battles, proofread my PowerPoints and handouts, think outside the box (and the prescribed curriculum), and laugh at myself because the kids surely will. Teachers are human as well. Certain things just come with the territory. The way a teacher acts and carries him or herself is a lesson in and of itself to students.

After speaking with and interacting with former students and having them see how I interact now with my current students, they all tell me how much I've changed. The main complaint I hear from the former students in relation to how I interact with the current students is, "You would have NEVER let us do this stuff!" I laugh it off and shrug and tell them that I'm just too old to do the stuff that I used to do with and to them. The reality is, the older I've gotten and the more students I've work with, the more I change to adapt to their needs.

In many regards, I didn't understand the types of students I was encountering. The issues they were facing and the behaviors they were exhibiting were things I had never before witnessed. I think I was too hard on them. Not only that, I think I was too hard on myself. I thought I had to be perfect for them. I thought that if I wasn't "hard" on them that they wouldn't take me seriously.

The truth is, I just needed to find a balance between firmness and fun. I needed to be myself and allow my personality to help shape my teaching and classroom management style. I needed to grow as an educator so that I could be the best I could for them without losing the essence of myself. I had to grow and mature into the position that would become my passion and my career.

YEAR 10 – IT REALLY WAS AN ACCIDENT

I had never been so excited to return to work after a summer break. Not that I didn't have a restful break, but I had a surprise for the students. They had been asking me all summer long whether I would or wouldn't be returning to the high school. I wasn't giving them any answers, so they had no idea I was coming back.

It was so wonderful to see how surprised they were when they realized I would be back. After all, the majority of the school's staff would be new to the building due to it being fresh started. I think they were glad to see a familiar face. Not only would I be staying, but I would move to 12th grade with them as their senior English teacher. Initially, I wasn't thrilled by the notion of teaching the same kids for the second year in a row, but in hindsight, it was probably the best thing that could have happened to and for us all.

It was at registration that they realized I was back. I received so much love from them. And I was only too pleased to return it. It was like a family reunion. Mama was home and she was excited to see her kids.

Not only would I be their senior English teacher, but I would also serve as a senior sponsor. In this role, I would once again help plan activities that students could participate in that would make their final year of high school the most memorable yet. For their first activity we took the students to take group photos in Downtown Memphis with the Mississippi River and the famed Memphis Bridge in the background. Afterward, we took them down historic Beale Street to the Hard Rock Café to eat lunch. And that's when it happened.

I had never been so embarrassed in my career. Prior to the event, the restaurant sent us menus to allow the students the opportunity to choose their meal ahead of time to make the serving process more efficient. But instead of efficiency, there was nothing but chaos.

I take for granted the fact that my son and I have gone to many different types of restaurants. I was able to teach him etiquette when it comes to ordering, speaking to wait staff, and tipping. I assumed that I didn't have to prep my students on proper restaurant behavior. I was utterly wrong.

Students were switching tables and confusing the wait staff. They were taking more servings than were allowed, stating they had not yet eaten. They were running in and out of the building. There were two young ladies who didn't even get to eat because eventually the kitchen staff stopped sending out plates as they had reached the maximum number of orders- keep in mind we sent orders in advance. It was complete chaos and I was livid.

Needless to say, news of the improper behavior made it back to school to the principal before we even arrived on campus. Once we arrived, we convened in the cafeteria where the principal made known her disappointment in the bad report. I, of course, had to add my thoughts as well. After all, the principal was new to the students. I expected them to test her. What I didn't expect was that they would test me. This was my second year with them. I had decided to come back to the school for them. And for them to disrespect me like that while we were in public after I had expressly told them to mind their manners? I would not have it!

Prior to this situation, the students had encouraged me to do a social media challenge that was popular at the time. The challenge was to remix the popular song "Bodak Yellow" by the rapper Cardi B. I had finished writing my version about a week prior to this incident, but their behavior gave my lyrics new meaning. And the Friday that we were dismissed for fall break, I recorded myself rapping the song and posted it to my Facebook page. What happened next was completely unimaginable.

The post garnered thousands of views, hundreds of shares and likes, hundreds of comments. I couldn't believe it. I was being called for interviews by local news media. I was asked to record the song at our school district's radio station and the song was played on the radio daily. I called my version of the song "Bodak Red" as red is one of the school's colors. "Bodak Red" was dubbed the 2017-2018 Senior Class Anthem. I was just doing it for my students. My greatest memory from that year was performing it at the homecoming pep rally with all my kids in the background hyping me up.

    Naturally, I'm a very shy person. I had come out of my box. My kids were quoting the lyrics to each other. They were quoting the lyrics to me. I had never done anything of that magnitude and never thought I would do anything of that nature again. The universe has a way of ensuring that you are in the right place at the right time for the right reasons.

    Later in the academic year, after returning to school after the holiday season, the weather took a turn for the worse and we got several inches of snow. In the minds of many, snow in Memphis is oxymoronic in a way. We tend to get more ice than anything. I guess the kids must have done a snow dance because snow is what we got.

Before the snow days, we had picked up some great momentum in our reading and discussion of *Guns, Germs, and Steel* by Jared Diamond. While reading the text, the students were attempting to answer and understand the premise question, "Why is it that white people were able to develop such advanced technology (cargo) and black and brown people were not?" They were really delving deep into the text when the snow came. During our time off, many of the students were still attempting to study and read the text on their own, but without my guidance, they became frustrated. It is this frustration that prompted one of my students to reach out to me via Facebook messenger to ask for assistance. What she asked changed my trajectory as a teacher forever.

She along with her peers requested that I go live over Facebook to teach a review lesson to ensure they were on the right path. I told her to get her peers together and set a time. I would get some notes together, so that we could do an in-depth review of the literature. I wanted to ensure that they understood the materials. What happened next was totally unexpected.

The next day, I logged on while still in my jammies and taught the best lesson I'd ever taught. Half of the senior class tuned in to view and ask questions. They also invited students from other schools to view the materials to get a better understanding. Members of the school board tuned in and praised me for going above and beyond the call of duty to ensure my kids received quality instruction. However, the best recognition of all came from my students as they thanked me and showed their appreciation for me taking time out to ensure they got the materials they needed. That's all I needed. Of course, it didn't end there.

Once again, I was interviewed by local news media and asked how it was that I decided to go out on a limb to teach the class a lesson via Facebook Live. I told the truth- had the children not requested it, it may not have happened. This time, however, there was much more publicity. I was interviewed by a syndicate of The Disney Chanel, Headline News, and several other national media outlets. I was shocked that a simple student request had garnered such a positive response. It was all because my kids took the initiative and used unconventional method to further their learning.

     Since I catered to their needs, I was recognized throughout the city as an exemplary educator. I was recognized at my district's Board of Education and I was awarded the MAT Educator Award by my alma mater, Christian Brothers University. I was also given the esteemed honor of being invited to my state's capital, Nashville, to receive recognition in the House of Representatives. The representative for the area in which I teach believed in me and my abilities. Since he respected the fact that my students regarded me in such high esteem, I now have a House Resolution in my name.

     I never set out to get any of the recognition that was given to me. All I wanted to do was let my kids know that I was there for them, no matter what they needed. It just so happened that people saw my genuine care for them and they rewarded me for doing what I love.

The Things I Learned – Year 10- Never forget that the students are ultimately in control of the learning environment.

Many teachers seem to think that classroom management and teaching are about control. You have to control the students. You have to control the lesson. You have to exert your authority and show that you are in charge of the situation to gain the respect of your students. But this is far from the truth.

I have learned that allowing the students to dictate and determine the direction of lessons is far more valuable than me trying to control everything. They will tell you what they want to and need to know. They will guide you in your instruction if you are willing to listen to them. You are a champion of their learning potential and that means relinquishing your need for control and allowing them to give you push back. It also means being flexible. Just because you make lesson plans doesn't mean that you have to stick to them verbatim.

I am a firm believer in the fluidity of lessons and the fact that lesson plans are living documents. Don't be rigid. Try new things. Allow the students the opportunity to give you some instruction when needed. Be open and willing to accept their feedback because you are in this profession to serve them. And the only way you can truly serve them is by allowing them to take the lead.

THE PRODIGAL STUDENT

I remember the first time I read the Parable of the Lost Son. I remember not understanding how the father could seemingly forsake the older son after he had done his best to obey his father's wishes. I remember being angry like the older son. I recall thinking to myself, "I can relate to him. I did well in school. I graduated from college. I never got in any major trouble when I was younger, yet my parents acted as though my accomplishments are meaningless. My younger sister and brother get all of this attention and here I am… Can't even get a pat on the back."

The older I get, the more I realize it was about the expectations. The father expected the older son to behave in a certain way because he always had. He could depend on that son. He seemed to worry more about the waywardness of the younger son. This is why that son was welcomed back with such praise and admiration. The father had a different expectation of that son's behavior. Not only that, but this was probably a son who was preached to and scolded until the father was blue in the face. He knew that this son would have to face life's lessons on his own.

I truly believe the father was proud that this son finally humbled himself and realized his wrongdoing. He didn't want to say, "I told you so;" he knew the young man had already been through too much. This story reminds me of a student I had several years ago. For the sake of anonymity, let's just call him Andrew.

I met Andrew when he was a freshman at the inner city school I was assigned to. From our initial conversations during the first weeks of school, I knew he was a bright young man. But as the quarter progressed, his behavior declined, the work he submitted was not of the same quality it had been initially, and he just (quite frankly) became a proverbial pain in the rear end.

He became an instigator and got suspended for fighting. He stopped being himself and started trying to fit in with students that seemed to mean him no good at all. Needless to say, I was so happy when he, in particular, was promoted to the next grade because I would be "rid" of him. Looking back on this, I am truly ashamed of how I felt about this boy.

I wouldn't have the pleasure of teaching him again until his junior year of high school. By this time, Andrew was a bit quiet and withdrawn. He didn't have the same liveliness of the boy I had met a year and a half prior. He was not himself at all, just a shell.

One day, after he had finished an assignment, he moved to a student desk that was near mine and began to confide in me. He had been having some personal issues within his family and the one person that he felt loved and cared for him was in ill health. He finally realized the life lessons that his loved one had instilled in him were valuable. He told me, "Ms. Brown, it's time for me to be a man. I have to make her proud." I was immediately in awe of this young man. Right before my eyes I saw him mature and begin to prioritize the things that were important to him. It was at this very moment that I could understand why the father in this parable was so excited to have his youngest son back. He was proud of his son's growth- proud of his maturation.

In your career, you will come across students who seem difficult, but this is only because they don't know how to react to life's hardships. Be mindful that although they may look grown, they may even want to be grown, but they are still, in essence, just children. They don't know or even understand how to handle all of life's situations and occurrences. There are some instances in which they just have to learn for themselves. But when they come back to you, welcome them with open arms. Be sincere in your approach to handling their return as this is the time when they will need you most.

BLESSINGS ON BLESSINGS

I remember being younger and going to church and there was always a portion of the service were the pastor would open up the floor to those who wanted to share with the congregation all of the ways that God had blessed them. These people would come to a secondary podium, give honor God, and pay their respects to the pastor and elders of the church before proceeding with their testimonies. These people would put their pride to the side and take that shame to the altar as they revealed the secrets that burdened them and how the love of God, coupled with repentance, brought them deliverance.

I always appreciated this portion of the weekly sermon because it was like a fresh start for those who needed it. No matter how things may have gone throughout the week, no matter how far a person may have strayed from the light of the Divine Creator, one could always speak to how he or she was brought back to the side of righteousness because God is love, God is light, and God is forgiveness.

No one has a perfect life. No one is without sin or blame. But there is one thing that I know for sure, those negative occurrences that take place in your life can be used as teachable moments and lessons for others. That's exactly what a testimony is. It is you using something that could have defeated you and flipping it so that it can be the driving force in your life so that you can become the best version of yourself.

Tests aren't easy. And you may not always know how you are going to overcome your valley moments. But those times of seeming darkness are actually blessings in disguise. They are the things that are going to shape you and make you better... if you allow them to.

I have come to accept and see the good that came from some of those negatives in my life. I have to if I want to receive blessings on blessings on blessings.

TESTIMONY

When I sit and think of all the things I've gone through since I began my teaching career, the only thing I can do is be thankful. I'm thankful to have chosen a career that allows me to be a parent. I'm thankful to have encountered so many students that I have been able to impact and learn from. I'm thankful that I still have relationships with many of those students and they know they can still call on me for advice if need be. I'm thankful for family and friends who have become my support system and allowed me to lean on them when things were too much for me to handle.

I have had some trying times in my life when I have wanted to give up and just walk away because things were too much to bear. But through it all I've continued to persevere and walk with my head held high. People have no idea how many times I've wanted to fight but, for fear of losing my child, I had to humble myself and walk away.

I've been alone, broken-hearted. I've been shunned and made to feel like less of a person- less of a teacher. Even now, I am being treated as though I have no place and no purpose in the building in which I work. But I've learned that the more people try to diminish your worth and value, the worthier and more valuable you actually are.

With some of the things I've gone through, I'm surprised I've endured this long. I'm surprised I've survived and not lost my mind. You must be built for this. And let me tell you, I'm built "Ford Tough."

You can't allow anyone to diminish your light, because that's exactly what it is. Being an educator is a calling, it's a ministry. And those who see that you are genuinely where you are supposed to be will do one of two things: they will either support you or they will tear you down.

In my years, I have been torn down more than I care to mention. I have been talked about, emotionally abused, and, when I tried to move on, harassed. It has only been recently, that is the last year, that people have been allowed to see what it really is I do and make judgments about me based on what they see and not hear. It is only recently that I have gained support.

I know that not everyone is going to be for me. And that is perfectly fine. But as long as I know my purpose, as long as I know who it is that I serve, as long as I know that I am doing and presenting my best daily, no one can be against me. And that is all that matters.

QUOTES AND SCRIPTURES

This final sections is composed of quotes and scriptures that I have referred back to constantly over the course of my career. These brief readings have given me the courage and strength to get out of the bed daily and stand at the front of a classroom full of kids and give them my best, even when I felt the world was against me.

My hope is that these jewels inspire others as much as they have inspired me. My hope is that people see the value in becoming an educator, as it is a very noble career. My hope is that people meditate on these things and see how they can be applied to real life- after all, as an educator, it is my job to show and prove to my students how the curriculum is applicable. Why would scripture be any different.

Luke 16:15

And he said unto them, Ye are they which justify yourselves before men; but God knoweth your hearts: for that which is highly esteemed among men is abomination in the sight of God.

    We all go through times in our lives in which we just want acceptance. We say to ourselves, "I hope such-and-such likes me," or, "I hope this person notices me today." We have all been there. This is even more so apparent in the life of an educator. No teacher wants to be the one that the students dislike. We don't want to be known as the mean one or the hard one. Not many of us take pride in being the one teacher whose class no student wants to take. However, what I've learned is that it doesn't matter what people think of you. If you mean well with your intentions, there is nothing bad anyone can say or think about you... well, at least not legitimately.

Depending on the grade you teach, you will see your students go through this phase as well. I have had the luxury, or the misfortune, of teaching 8th through 12th grade English and Language Arts. Believe me when I say, I have seen peer pressure and students trying to fit in at many different age levels and in many different forms.

As an educator, you must understand that school is not just a place for academic exploration. School is also a mechanism for honing social skills. They learn about friendship and betrayal. They experience first crushes, love, and heartache. These truly are the formative years of a person's life. The things they experience during this time shape their behaviors as an adult. This is the time when fitting in matters the most.

What I've seen is that no one wants to be the outsider. So what kids typically do is cling to someone or to some group that seems to be the "most" of what they desire. The most outgoing, the most intelligent, the most original, the most talented, the most recognized. Just the "most" whether that thing be positive or negative. These kids truly just desire attention and many of them want it without regard to which type they receive. It is because of this that this scripture speaks to me. These are people who truly justify themselves and their actions by the crowd in which they associate. What they do is ok because there are others that are participating in the same activities. But how many times have we all heard the familiar adage, "If your friends jumped off a bridge, would you do it too?" And this is what I think of here.

You can't justify what you do before man. Humans are not always good judges of character. Not only this, but there is also the fact that many people behave one way around their group of friends and then are completely different when they are outside of that circle. Isn't that interesting? You'd think that they would be the same all around, but it is a matter of fitting in. It is a matter of wanting to belong. They aren't mature enough to realize that it is not the people around them who will be their biggest critics—it is their conscience.

    It is my honest belief and opinion that the conscience is that bit of God that resides in us. At the end of the day, man may view your actions one way, but God sees things completely differently. What is accepted by man is not always accepted by God. When we know and understand this, it is easy to forgive the foolish ways of the students we teach (and possibly even the foolish ways of some of our colleagues).

In the same light, realizing this for our own lives, we will begin doing things for integrity's sake as opposed to gaining recognition because let's face it, we are a part of a group that day in and day out does a job that is THANKLESS!

Let's do things because they are acceptable in the eyes of The Lord. Man's acceptance is neither desired nor required to get the job done to the best of our abilities.

Luke 15:7

I say unto you, that likewise joy shall be in heaven over one sinner that repenteth, more than over ninety and nine just persons, which need no repentance.

Okay, I say to you that there are going to be times and lessons that you truly ask yourself, "Am I speaking a foreign language? Why don't they get it?" You can film yourself for critique, you can have someone else come in and advise you. But I'm here to tell you, that chances are, it ain't you!

Sometimes, things just click for different students at different times. There are students that will get the concepts on the first try. There are some students that you may have to reteach the concepts before it makes sense to them. But there are some that no matter what you do, the concept will just go right over their heads. Now that doesn't mean you give up on them. It just means you must come up with more creative ways for them to grasp the concept so that it becomes real to them.

Let me tell you, when that one student who has been struggling the entire lesson is finally able to explain the concept in a way that makes sense not only to him/herself but to you and the rest of the class as well, you celebrate that student more than you did any of the other students that seemed to grasp it on the first try. It's the same feeling as that of the Prodigal Son. You have to celebrate the moment!

You will have a sense of joy and pride that you never thought possible. You will boast and brag on that student and he or she will be so excited and overjoyed. Let that student have his or her moment in glory. Your praise over him or her will quite possibly be the thing that sparks a life-long love of learning.

There is always more joy in the one person that is struggling getting it right than the student who seems to get everything the first try. Now, with that being said, you shouldn't overlook the students who do typically grasp the concepts quickly. Praise them as well. Give them duties and jobs that will boost their confidence as well. Allow them to tutor or be the teacher's assistant. This will show them that you have recognized their hard work and efforts as well.

Proverbs 9:6

Forsake the foolish, and live; and go in the way of understanding.

Some battles aren't meant to be fought. Some arguments aren't meant to be engaged in. You never want someone to question which is the fool. Who wants to wear egg on their face?

As an educated individual, it should be easy to pick your battles. However, when you are dealing with students who are allowed to question everything- students who are not often held accountable for their actions or words but will try to hold everything you say and do against you, it can be really easy to "lose your cool." We all fall victim to that one student who must make everything an argument. He or she must always have the last word and must always be right. Don't let that student be your downfall. Realize that you are in a professional position. Some things should be left alone because at the end of the day, grades are due, and conduct grades are at your discretion.

There will be battles that you must fight. There will be wars in which you must engage; don't become engaged in the wrong sort of conflict. You will waste a good fight on the useless while leaving the deserving undefended.

Proverbs 12:1

Whoever loves discipline loves knowledge, but whoever hates correction is stupid.

Now this is not to say that any child or adult is stupid. But we can only learn and grow if we recognize our mistakes and if we accept the criticism that helps us to correct our areas of weakness. Remember that we are indeed human beings. Human beings make mistakes. What we do with those mistakes determines our character.

We have all heard the old adage, "If at first you don't succeed, you must try and try again." And this definitely holds true. What could make this even better is if there is someone there to help you to identify the mistakes you made that prevented your initial success. We all need help at some point. We shouldn't be so foolish and prideful as to not accept constructive criticism from those who sincerely want to see us succeed. With that being said, we all know that there are people who will criticize us in hopes of tearing us down to make themselves feel better. These are the types of people you must quickly remove from your life.

In this profession, it is better to work with a partner as opposed to going at it alone. I remember very well my feelings my first year in the classroom. I was inexperienced and had no support from anyone. I was exhausted and stressed beyond measure. The people that should have been there to help me and guide me through the process were trying their hardest to stifle any growth I could have possibly experienced because I didn't commit to their "agenda."

Let me tell you, the Devil is alive and well in all aspects. People will commit themselves to tearing you down just to say that they knew you would fail. They will claim they knew you weren't strong enough to handle the pressure. Push all of that aside and know that God is a comforter. He is there as a counselor and a friend. Ask Him for guidance and wisdom in whatever situation you may face on your journey today. Don't wait! Don't be foolish and prideful and think that you can handle this on your own. The classroom is a very stressful place to be if you don't have the support you need to be successful.

Allow yourself to be corrected. Allow a knowledgeable person to give you pointers on how to work efficiently and effectively. Don't be ashamed to ask for assistance. There is no condemnation in saying that you are overwhelmed and need help. At the same time, you can't just ask these things of anyone. Ask God to allow people in your life that are truly there to be of encouragement. Ask God to guide you, to lead you, to direct you on the path of righteousness as you undertake His calling in the classroom because it truly is a calling on your life. Don't let your pride deter you from being the best educator that you can be; you are here to make a difference and you will need all the help you can get in order to do so.

Deuteronomy 8:3

And he humbled thee, and suffered thee to hunger, and fed thee with manna, which thou knewest not, neither did thy fathers know; that he might make thee know that man doth not live by bread alone, but by every word that proceedeth out of the mouth of the Lord doth man live.

Sometimes we must endure tough times so that we can acknowledge that we still have more growing to do. We must realize that this is a profession that many are not equipped to handle. You are of the minority. No one will understand your plight unless they have been in your shoes and worn the hat of an educator. Don't take it personally that no one understands. Also, don't take it lightly that no one understands. It is a humbling experience to know that you have a hand in shaping the life of a child and guiding his or her future in the way of integrity just as God was trying to guide Israel despite its stubbornness.

There will be times that you truly want to give up and walk away from this profession. I've been there too many times to count, but in the end, I always return. The students I teach humble me. They show me that I really don't know and understand everything. They teach me something new every time I enter the classroom. They show me there is more to life than what I was taught in my education courses. There is more in being an educator than the theories and strategies I was taught to use in order to engage them. I must continue to hunger for knowledge and wisdom. I must keep an open mind, heart, and spirit so that I can truly understand their needs and wants.

Not everyone has the privileges that I have had. Not everyone shares my experiences. And this is what an educator must understand about his or her teaching situation. Just as Abraham's experience with God was completely different from that of his son, so our life experiences are different from those we teach. This doesn't make anyone else's situation any better or worse for wear, but it does imply growth on one's individual journey. Hunger for God's guidance so that he can use you to shape and minister to His children in the way that He needs you too.

Psalms 27:4

One thing that I desire of the Lord and that will I seek after; that I may dwell in the house of the Lord all the days of my life, to behold the beauty of the Lord, and to enquire in his temple.

    There truly is beauty in teaching and educating children. Your desire should be to encourage growth. To encourage students to become better versions of themselves... We have a goal.

    We want the kids to leave us better than when they came. God wants that overall for our lives. Our encounter with Him should change every aspect of our lives for the better. Truth be told, we are stewards of The Lord, and we should have the same effect on every life that crosses the threshold to enter our learning environment. They should thirst for and desire knowledge and wisdom just as we thirst for and the desire the presence of The Lord who is wisdom and knowledge incarnate.

Philippians 4:6-7

Be careful for nothing; but in everything by prayer and supplication with Thanksgiving let your requests be made known to God. And the peace of God, which passeth all understanding shall keep your hearts and minds through Christ Jesus.

Pray daily. Thank God daily. Ask for renewal of mind, body, and spirit daily. Know and understand that you have a daunting task before you, but allow God to guide you in every aspect.

Ask Him to open the minds of your students so that they are receptive to you. Ask Him to give you the appropriate words so that you may effectively reach each student. Ask Him to BRIDLE YOUR TONGUE when those moments of frustration come about because for the life of you, you can't understand how

Susie didn't understand that concept when you made it easy as pie!

There is nothing too mundane or too extraordinary for God to handle. The more you give over to Him, the more peace you will have within yourself and in your career.

Numbers 6:24-26

The Lord bless thee and keep thee: The Lord make his face shine upon thee and be gracious unto thee: The Lord lift up his countenance upon thee and give thee peace.

    This prayer has been on my mind and in my heart since the first time I read it. I've actually been thinking of making this prayer a part of my morning routine with my son because it is just so powerful. This prayer is all about the goodness and mercy of The Lord.

    Remain in God's presence. Don't shut Him out during this time. The career you are embarking upon, whether you're a novice or a seasoned veteran, is not for the faint of heart. Allow God to come in to you. Invite the presence of the Holy Spirit into your classroom, your mind, your heart. Ask the Father for strength and courage during this time. Ask Him to give you the words you will need to capture the attention of the students and engage them in meaningful work. Allow Him to move you where He deems fit. Being an educator during this particular time is very trying. You cannot do this alone. You need to put on the whole armor of God and trust that He will keep you.

    Accept God's grace and know that you aren't deserving of it. Remain humble and thankful. In this career, you are going to make a lot of mistakes. It just comes with the territory. You can't go into a classroom and think you have all the answers. After almost a decade in the classroom, I can honestly say I don't have all the answers. Each new school term brings its own issues and situations. No matter how much I think I have prepared, there is always a new way to do things and that also comes with the territory. Be flexible. Admit when you make mistakes. Apologizing doesn't hurt as much as you think it does. And always know and understand that tomorrow is a new day to try new things, to try to improve upon your skills. Keep in mind that this is just as much a learning experience for us as it is for the students.

Ask God to bless all of the endeavors you plan to embark upon during this school year. Prayer is not only a means of asking God for something, it is also His way of giving you peace and permission to do things. Before I became a teacher, I asked God if this was something that I was supposed to do. Even now, after almost 10 years, I ask God to bless my lessons and any ideas I have that I think will better help my students understand concepts. I ask God to give me ideas and fresh perspective so that I can ensure that I am meeting my students where they are. I may not be the most effective on a daily basis, but I always pray that on any given day my kids take away something useful.

Allowing God to move in your life during this time and not shutting Him out will give you the peace you need to endure any and every circumstance that could occur this year. Again, this is not a task you can embark upon on a whim. You must be strong and courageous to undertake the feat of educating today's youth. As a good friend of mine once told me, "This is a calling. Although you may feel ill-equipped you must remember- God may not always call those who are equipped for the job, but He will always equip those He has called."

Genesis 1:1-3

In the beginning God created the heaven and the earth. And the earth was without form and void; and darkness was upon the face of the deep. And the spirit of God moved upon the face of the waters. And God said, "Let there be light." And there was light.

You create the learning environment you want. Be as creative and uplifting as you want. The only limitation should be the size of your classroom, nothing else. Research and find things that could possibly work for the level in which you teach. You're the creator of the climate and culture within your domain. Make it conducive to your personality and what you expect from your students and relay these expectations to your students.

2 Thessalonians 3:10

For even when we were with you, this we commanded you, that if any would not work, neither should he eat.

You are not obligated to reward idleness, laziness, or foolishness. Students who put forth no effort should get grades that reflect that. As a teacher, your expectation should be that all students try and at least attempt the work you give. This helps you gauge their understanding and plan accordingly. However, if no attempt is made (i.e. there is no work being done) no grade should be given (no food should be given). That is only fair. After all, would you be given a paycheck if you didn't come in and do your job? Same concept.

Joyce Meyer

"God gave us emotions for more purposes than just being enthusiastic at a ball game or about a new car. Surely God wants us to employ our emotions in expressing our love and gratitude to Him... If we had a proper emotional release during praise and worship, we might not release emotions at other times in improper ways."

In order to be in this profession, you have to make emotional connections. No matter how much you say you will not get close to students, there is always that one kid that makes you break down those emotional barriers so that you connect with him or her on a more personal level. This has happened to me so many times over the years.

I often wonder why I seem to be the one teacher that usually has this sort of connection with the students. People always say that no one else seems to connect with them the way that I do. To this day, students still contact me for help or advice and I always hope and pray that I guide them in the right direction.

Maybe this is the gift that God has given me. I often believe that it is part of my calling into this ministry. I never thought I would ever be sensitive to the emotional needs of others, but apparently, I am continually being bestowed with the wherewithal.

God has given us emotions so that we can adequately give him glory and praise. The anger and frustration we often feel in this profession means that we need to get closer to him. When we are closer to him, our emotions are stable, and we can see clearly and logically how to react to certain situations and circumstances. I typically call on him in some form or fashion to guide me during times like these.

Yearly. Monthly. Weekly. Daily. We need renewal. We need to renew our focus. We need to renew our emotions. I believe that this is the reason fellowship is so important. Not only is fellowship with other likeminded believers important, but also fellowship with and connection to the Holy Spirit is a necessity. When we are in connection with the Holy Spirit and truly releasing our emotions from the depth of our own spirit, we feel a sort of alignment with God.

When our spiritual lives are aligned with God, the emotions we release are also aligned with him. The things we feel can either overwhelm us and deter us or they can influence us and help us grow. With God's guidance, we can react in ways that are not only for our good but also for the good of others.

Deuteronomy 31:6

Be strong and of good courage, fear not, nor be afraid of them: for the Lord thy God, he it is that doth go with thee; he will not fail thee, nor forsake thee.

    I haven't met a teacher yet that didn't feel some sort of fear on a daily basis when entering the classroom. But as many people know, to display fear in the classroom is a big mistake. The kids are like bees- they smell fear! I'm only kidding- maybe. But the truth is this is a profession in which you must be spiritually and emotionally strong. Physical strength is not the key here. There is a bit of finesse that must be displayed and applied. It is because of this that your spiritual, emotional, and physical strength must be in top performing condition.

The Lord will be with you during this arduous journey, if you ALLOW Him to be. The Lord will guide and keep you during this time, if you ALLOW Him to do so. This is a thankless job in which you will be disrespected, paid poorly, and treated as though your degrees are worthless. You must be slightly crazy and all brave in order to accept the task at hand and come to work day in and day out knowing that you will face those things.

Recognize and understand that although you feel that way, there are still those who look up to you. The students will be the bane of your existence and the source of your joy. And sometimes those two things will happen in the same day, possibly even the same class period. Be thankful for your role in their lives. You are there for a purpose even if the season is short-lived.

When you have days that you feel you want to give up, just remember what Moses told Joshua. Joshua was Moses' successor. He was the one that would lead the Israelites to the Promised Land as Moses was told that he would not experience the joy thereof. As their former leader, Moses knew that there would be days that Joshua would experience things that would frighten him; he knew that there would be days that Joshua would want to give up; he knew that there would be days that Joshua would not feel God's presence as much as other days.

However, in all of these things, Moses tells him to be strong and courageous and to not show fear. Moses reassures him that God is with him always, and if God is with him, he can accomplish anything. Moses assures Joshua that God's presence will never leave him, nor will God forsake him when His presence is needed the most.

I am here to tell you to receive the same advice that was given to Joshua. There will be times over the course of your career, over the course of the school year, over the course of the semesters, over the course of the months, over the course of the weeks, over the course of the days that you will feel extreme discontent and extreme discourage. Look to God during those times. Just call on His name. He will hear you and renew your strength. I assure you He will.

James 1:2-3

My brethren, count it all joy when ye fall into divers temptations; knowing this, that the trying of your faith worketh patience.

With all of the instances of students disrespecting teachers by talking back, cursing them out, and destroying private property, it's a true wonder that many more teachers have not begun to leave the profession sooner. But we know this is a calling. We know the about the communities we are venturing into and the demographics we will encounter. We know what we are getting ourselves into. Of course, there is always a bit of naiveté in the beginning, but a good teacher, one who is invested in the outcome, researches the backgrounds of his or her students to ensure that he or she is effective and relatable.

This does not, however, mean that we are superman or superwoman. We are human. There are times when James talks back that we are going to want to give him a piece of our mind. There is going to be a time when Jessica tries to test your patience by pulling out her phone and selfie stick in your class during the middle of a lesson and it is going to take everything in you to remember that you are a professional with degrees.

You are going to be tempted to react. But many of the actions of the students don't require a reaction. As young people, they want to see how far they can push the boundaries. In my career, the reason that many students push back when it comes to authority and rules is that they aren't required to follow any except during the time they are at school. Is this right? No. Is this reality? Yes.

How can you truly instill a need for following and abiding by rules at school when the students think school is pointless? These kids have real issues. They have been raped and beaten. They are taking care of younger siblings while mom is gone for days and weeks at a time and dad is nowhere to be found. They are taking care of their own kids at home but expected to remain "in a child's place" between the hours of 7:15am and 2:15pm. Not only is it hard for them, but it is hard for us as well.

We can't allow the enemy to tempt us into behaving in a way that is out of our character. We must remember that we were once teenagers. We were lost and needed guidance although we didn't know it. We once thought we were invincible and above reproach. With experience comes wisdom. Since the students we teach have varying levels of life experience, we cannot place them all in a single category. We must be patient and willing to get to know and understand them. Once we do that, we can then educate them.

    Be thankful for the temptations, it will teach you to more readily ask The Father for guidance. It will teach you to bridle your tongue. It will teach you to pick your battles. It will teach you to be more observant. It will teach you to value your students' experiences. It will help you to become a better educator.

2 Corinthians 5:7

For we live by faith and not by sight.

It is not always clear whether or not our students actually listen to us as we stand at the front of the class pouring our hearts and souls out during our lessons. We act it out and perform for them. We do these things, so they can see our passion in hopes that they too will eventually be passionate about the subject matter.

Sadly, it doesn't always work. We have to have faith and know and understand that what we are doing is reaching even one person.

Galatians 6:9

As you teach, do not get tired of doing what is good. At just the right time you will reap a harvest of blessings.

At the time that I am writing this, I have just completed my tenth year in the classroom. Ten first days of school. Ten last days of school. Ten testing seasons. Hundreds of students. I can't tell you how many times I've questioned my effectiveness and the validity of my methodology in the classroom. I am constantly reflecting over my practices to ensure that I am doing what the students need and sometimes, I feel like I come up short and let them down.

However, every time I wanted to give up or I thought I was faltering, there was always a student that that assured me that I was doing a good job and that I was on the right path. He or she always showed me why I should stay. This student always made me feel as though there was no other teacher in the building that could do what I do. And so, I would wipe my face and ask God to guide me and show me if this was where I needed to be. Inevitably, The Higher Power would answer me in the affirmative- so I'd stay and endure.

I say all of that to let you know that there will be some turbulent times as you navigate your way through the year. This is not a profession for someone who is looking for an easy way out. But it is definitely the most rewarding journey I have ever been on. Stay the course. Of course, there are days when you will be weary, and you will feel as though you have tried everything to get through to your students. Try once more. When you least expect it, your students will show you why your hard work wasn't for naught.

Find a buddy on your hall or be sure to have a trusted confidant outside of your workspace so that you can vent your frustrations. But VENT, don't GRIPE. Sometimes hearing yourself is the best way to come up with ideas that could benefit your students.

Not only that, having someone to listen to you is therapeutic. Get it all out and then go back in there and give it your all. Your kids deserve your best. And whether you feel it or not, you are exactly what at least one of them needs. Everything you do, do it with them in mind. Show them. Guide them. Direct them. Don't ever get tired of putting their needs first. You may just be the only person in their lives to do this for them. And when the time is right, they will show you just how much you mean to them. They will show off just how much they learned from you. Remember, you reap what you sow.

1 Peter 5:6

So humble yourselves under the mighty power of God, and at the right time he will lift you up in honor.

In order to be a great teacher, you first have to be a great student. The 2017-2018 school year taught me that humility is such a blessing. During the school year, I gained quite a bit of notoriety. In October 2017, I made an educational remix to a popular rap song and it became the anthem for the senior class. I was featured in the local news media and even had the opportunity meet the artist who created the original song.

Then, in January 2018, as we were just coming back from winter break, we had another week out due to snow and hazardous road conditions. One of my students requested a lesson be taught over live streaming (Facebook) and I was only too happy to accommodate. It started off rocky as my sister and my son made cameo appearances. I was frustrated because I didn't know if my students could hear or see me. But I got it done.

I had never done either of these things before. I'm not a rapper. I'm actually very shy and don't like to be photographed, let alone filmed. The things I had done were held in such high esteem that my work garnered national attention by way of CNN Headline News. But not one time did I let those things go to my head. If anything, the attention made me fearful that those things would become part of what people expected from me. I was only doing my job. And I was doing it in a way that my kids could relate.

I say all of that to say this, we all have great ideas and moments of success. But just as we have successes, we are prone to failures. Don't allow success to make you forget where you come from. The things I did were not to gain fame or glory from outsiders. I only did the rap because I knew that I could get the attention of my students. I only did the live streamed lesson at the request of my students. And when the cameras were gone, it back to business as usual. The residual attention that I gained throughout the district only allowed people to get a glimpse of the type of person and educator I really am. That attention has put me on the path to something bigger. I don't yet know what that something bigger is, but I do know that it will be revealed when the time is right.

You may not have a year like I had where you are thrust into the public eye, but you are in the public eye nonetheless. Remember that your true goal is to educate students, not show off how smart or how great you think you are. The education that you provide to these kids will speak to your intelligence and greatness. Humility is a beautiful quality to possess. Know that just as quickly as you become recognized is as quickly as people can forget who you are. The real reward is the growth we get to witness as our students grow and mature from children into young adults.

CLOSING REMARKS AND CANDID MOMENTS

I do hope that I have shed some light on the things that take place in the classroom that can make and shape educators. Of course, we all have our own individual, unique experiences that that mold us. But more often than not, all educators go through similar themes of highs and lows. It's all about how you handle the situation. And if there's one thing I've learned it's to bend but not break.

In closing, I leave for your enjoyment some candid moments from several points in my career. It is my hope that the love and passion I possess for these kids has been expressed adequately in the pages of this book.

Peace and Blessings.

This photo was taken right before we marched out on that rainy day in May 2012 for commencement activities. I was so relieved to be done. The only thing I was worried about was whether or not they would pronounce my name correctly. I was so relieved that all of my hard work had paid off. I was officially going to have a teaching license!

Those who know me know that I love Halloween and costumes. So why wouldn't I share that love with my students? I was sad that so few of them participated in the festivities, but I still had an awesome time. I truly believe that there is no reason to not let your personality shine in the classroom. Yes, you are the teacher. But who said teachers can't have fun?

Photo Credit- Supriya Ward

The young man standing beside me in this photo is nothing short of amazing. He and I were both invited to the State House of Representatives to receive awards. My work was done in the classroom and community. His was done in the classroom and on the football field where he broke school, district, and state records. I am so proud to say that he is now a college student that is still setting records on the field. But I am even more proud that he has achieved academic honors!

I must say I give the meanest side eye this side of the Mississippi! I am 95% certain I was fussing the moment this image was captured. But it's all in love!

From the moment I met these two during their junior year of high school, I knew they would give me a run for my money. And I wasn't wrong! As much as they pushed me, I also pushed them and they were made better for it as they are both working and in school and focused on pursuing their dreams.

Teaching middle school was by far one of the toughest points in my career. But I will say this, the parents of middle schoolers must know the struggle because they give the BEST Teacher Appreciation gifts! I don't think that cupcake or strawberry made it to my car that day!

With the popularity of my remix of a popular rap song came some major responsibility. I was asked to perform the song at the homecoming pep rally for our football team, which was undefeated at the time. No pressure at all right? Wrong! I was so nervous. I'm not a performer at all. So when the music came on, I looked behind me at my students and said, "Please don't make me do this alone!" And they did not disappoint! They made the performance better than I could have ever thought possible! I am so pleased to have this as a memory!

Photo Credit- Mr. Kever Conyers

ABOUT THE AUTHOR

Candous Brown, an 11-year veteran of the classroom, resides in Memphis, TN where she has taught English Language Arts, Etymology, and Mythology to students in grades 8-12. Her educational background in English Literature, coupled with pedagogical strategies, has given her the tools necessary to reach and teach the diverse groups of students who have entered her classroom over the years. Her effectiveness in the classroom has been recognized by her peers who nominated her for Educator of the Year, by her State Representatives who awarded her a House Resolution, and by the education department at

Christian Brothers University (BA and MAT) which awarded her the Outstanding M. A. T. Educator Award for 2018. When Candous is not educating and mentoring the city's youth, she enjoys reading, traveling, and spending time with her son. You can learn more about Candous and her experiences in the classroom at https://mscsbrown12.wixsite.com/website.

EDUCATION AND PROFESSIONAL CREDENTIALS

Millington Central High School 2003: Diploma

Christian Brothers University 2007: Bachelor of Arts in English

Christian Brothers University 2012: Master of Arts in Teaching

Aspiring Teacher Leader

Photo Credits

Title Page Image

Photo Credit: Caroline Bauman

Cover and About the Author Image

Photo Credit: Brandon Morgan